DIGGING DEEPER

Reflections in Wisdom

CHASTINE ROCK

DIGGING DEEPER

Reflections in Wisdom

Chastine Rock

ISBN (Print Edition): 978-1-66782-194-8

ISBN (eBook Edition): 978-1-66782-195-5

DEDICATION

I dedicate this book to my wife, who has always shined forth as the light of God in our house. She's always the music that is never playing from an instrument, but from the heart. She's brought forth our children in the same atmosphere that she herself dwells in and is given her life to shine on the shadows of others that they may see how to take wise steps in life. Proverbs 3:13-26, describes her, *"For wisdom is like a good wife and the many things that shine forth from that relationship."* I also dedicate this book to the prophetic phrase that my uncle Mutt spoke to me when I was younger. That phrase, *"dig deeper"*, has been with me through these spiritual years of insight, teaching, and living the life. Our children serve the Lord as a light that my wife shined in our home that they were transformed through. They are very instrumental in all of the ministry work that we do now.

To all the teachers, ministers and prophetic workers in the Body of Christ that have shared their wisdom with us throughout these many years, I call you all blessed, and definitely favored by our Lord Jesus Christ. May these phrases of wisdom reach into the hearts of men and women that are seeking to live life above the ordinary.

Amen,

Apostle Chastine M. Rock

DAY 1

"The Benefits of Obedience"

Whenever people strive to withdraw from obedience, they have forfeited the presence of God's grace. Adam was sent from Eden, because of disobedience, which is a spreading sin. That spreading sin has come to all mankind, and all have disobeyed. But Jesus has redeemed us, and now obedience, is our road to joy. Job 36:11, *"If they obey and serve him, they shall spend their days in prosperity, and their years in pleasures."* Sounds like a winner to me. Study Matthew 7:24–25, as you dig deeper.

☙DAY 2❧

"A Perfect Copycat"

Accoording to Scripture, the eyes of faith always see the victory. The eyes of faith powers our way through negative reports, and even negative circumstances to victory on the other side. Faith sees the situation, and doesn't deny it, but says what the Word of God says about the situation. True faith declares situational change. If what you say with your mouth is the result of what has been seeded in your heart, then your faith will work for you. Just make sure the seed is God's Word and nothing else. Stop wasting your time following parked people, they're not going anywhere. Study Hebrews 6:12, and dig deeper.

⚘DAY 3⚘

"The Perfect Copycat"
Part 2

By now you should have read Hebrews 6:12, so sit back and grab this. We are cautioned not to love ease, because it will cause loss of opportunities, and loss of opportunities hinder success. If you are going to be the perfect copycat, copy something big, because our God is too big for us to be small. Study Galatians 5:13-26, and dig deeper.

❦DAY 4❦

"Why Research?"

S incere Bible readers know that Matthew 6:33, is the key that opens the doors to our divine storehouse of blessings. We need to understand what it is to, *"seek first the Kingdom of God"*, and then allow the manifestation of the resources of the Kingdom to come into our life. Seek means to ask, making a diligent inquiry, and walking in constant pursuit of God. To search for how God does things, and His way of thinking will require perseverance. Sounds like fun doesn't it? Let's start with Psalms 34:8-10, while we dig deeper.

DAY 5

"Why Research?"
Part 2

Seek first the way God does things. Walking in His ways, is the pattern to improve your life. Some people think that their family is first, and God is second. Family is important, but family can't bring the power and blessings of heaven on you, unless that family is walking under the divine order of heaven, then generational blessings can flow from that family. That's not the case with most families, and many place family before God, which is totally ridiculous. Research the Lord God, for He has promised to always be near those that seek Him. Study Isaiah 46:8-11, and help someone else dig deeper.

DAY 6

"Why Research?"
Part 3

Some may think that because they gave their life to the Lord at one time or another in our life, that that makes them a God seeker. One thing can be said for unbelievers and that is, they earnestly seek worldly things. If you want to see what it means to diligently seek something, just watch how most people go to work every day, whether they like the job or not. They go regardless of the conditions of their health, the weather, and of their pay, they go. Study John 7:37-38, and dig deeper.

DAY 7

"Why Research?"
Part 4

Some may think, what if I spend time seeking God and nothing happens? If that's the case, please read on. What you're thinking is an impossible event, because if you come near to God with your heart, you never see Him standing at a distance. James 4:8, will clear up that dark picture in your thinking. God is interested in a receiver, one that can hold the impossible, grow the dream, and spread the grace. Study 2 Chronicles 16:9, as you dig deeper.

᭐DAY 8᭐

"Why Research?"
Part 5

It's never too late to seek the Kingdom of God. No, you haven't missed your chance, nor your time. Why not? Because, God knows your heart. Your thoughts are words to Him, and He hears every conversation. What's more, no matter how much trouble or hell you've raised, God has a plan to get you over any obstacle, any delay, or any barren season. He's always so loving that it's hard to comprehend at times, so don't stop researching. Read Jeremiah 29:11-14 and dig deeper.

❧DAY 9❧

"Faith Always Wins"

Some people are reluctant to put God first, because they are afraid of what the Lord may ask them to do. If you're one of those, let me assure you, there's nothing to fear. When you seek the Lord first, what you find is His goodness and blessings. Even if He tells you something that's hard on your flesh, you will be glad you obeyed, because that obedience will open up the door of favor for you. Study Deuteronomy 28:1-2, as you dig deeper.

❧ DAY 10 ❧

"The "Ifs" of Life"

No matter what circumstances you face, God can turn them around. I've heard people say, that if this or that had been different, life would have been different. When you focus on the "If's", you can hinder your future success of faith. Jesus always focused on what He had, not what He didn't. If you are a believer, the "Ifs" actually give you a great opportunity to prove that the Word of God works. You can organize your defeat into victory, again I repeat, you can organize your defeat into victory. Hope you got that! Study John 11:21-40, as you dig deeper.

DAY 11

"Love is Forever"

As we grow up in the Lord, we discover that God's love grows in our hearts. Why? Because, the love we have, we have received from Him. The growing of that love takes some effort, like growing a garden, we must put some effort to it. If we want a harvest from that love, we must keep our hearts soft, not hard, but soft so that the supernatural love can grow unhindered. Study John 15, the whole chapter, as you dig deeper.

✌️DAY 12✌️

"Together as One"

The Scriptures emphasize how much more we can accomplish through cooperating with others. Psalms 133 has been a statement that cries loud for every generation. We must never forget that God has ordained the church in such a way that we need each other for effectiveness. That effectiveness increases when we join together in unity. If every believer did his or her part to effectively increase the body, how many more great ministries could have great stories that give God glory? Study Leviticus 26:8, as you dig deeper.

 DAY 13

"Supernatural Supply"

The sheer volume of provision God gave to Israel in the wilderness journey should help your faith in receiving from God. It was an unfailing supply of manna every day. Millions of souls were satisfied, each and every day with six pints of manna. That was over 18 million pints a day, and over 7 tons by weight every day. Today we could pack 15 trains, each having 30 boxcars, with each holding 15 tons. Yet, you're wondering if God can get you through? Study Psalms 145 and keep on digging deeper.

✺DAY 14✺

"Moving Up and Out of Situations"

Isaiah 40:31, gives a perfect picture of how we have victory over circumstances. While we wait, we march forward in faith. We don't fold, we hold to faith. We don't sit and do nothing, for we are World Overcomers. Our faith can turn barren wastelands into fruitful meadows, and broken-down cities, into places of great grace. Just ask Hannah, who was barren in the physical, but was fruitful in the spiritual. Study 1 Samuel Chapter 1 and continue to dig deeper. For there's wisdom waiting to be received in the Scriptures.

⚝DAY 15⚝

"The Proper Position"

No leader can carry out God's plan alone. He needs the help of others, willing to work in unity, and committed to the local church. Why? Because, it takes everyone together to get the results that bring glory to God, and the benefit of that work within the people will be the great manifestation of God's goodness toward us. Wisdom would always want you to know and realize that you are important to God's plan for the church, and that there's a place that no one else but you can fill. 1 Corinthians 12:12-31 is a great place to dig deeper.

✌️DAY 16✌️

"Helping at the Bottom of the Mountain"

O n the Mount of Transfiguration, Peter wanted to stay right there, he said so. It's not good to rest at the top, because help is needed at the bottom. Don't let the Son-ship role make you a spiritual hermit. Once you grasp the secret of this high calling in Christ Jesus, you must also know that there are others that haven't been to the top yet. None of the believers in the lower realm could fix this desperate human situation that was among them. That's why you must return to the bottom, because none of those believers that were in that lower realm had any answers that could fix that desperate situation. Wisdom would always have us to remember where we came from, and that others are still there waiting for light to come to them. Dig deeper into Matthew 7:1-21, as we step into more wisdom.

⚘DAY 17⚘

"It's Not Over"

In Mark 5:21-43, there is a picture of a new beginning when an end seems to be in place. Jairus is on his way home with Jesus, and the news of his daughter's death greets him. The death of the child does not put an end to the narrative. Why not? Because, Jesus encouraged him to believe what he had first believed. Our way of thinking is that while we live, there is room for hope. Jesus' way of thinking is that He is your hope regardless of the situation. Regardless of what it looks like, the wisdom of God speaks to us and tells us that all things, and I mean all things, are possible with God. Keep digging deeper.

❧ DAY 18 ❧

"It's Not Over"
Part 2

As mentioned in the earlier wisdom lesson, at the death of someone our hope ends, because life is gone, it is past recalling. Those dead do not have power to rise, therefore, the picture we see in this particular lesson is the power of the Lord that goes along with His word to make it effectual. Our Lord works while He commands, and works by command, therefore He can command whatever He pleases. Don't get stuck in the picture of a situation, but let your heart be deep and embedded into the nature of our Lord. His will is to deliver you from whatever is causing life to be a disappointment.

❧DAY 19❧

"The Real Deal"

You can count on a battle-ready Christian. Why? Because, we are heavenly beings, we are partakers of an ascended lifestyle given through the glory of God. God has placed us in orbit around His will, with the new perspective of life in Christ Jesus, and we are now downloaded with His anointing every day to influence, and to give away this spiritual life. Nothing in the lower world can cast a shadow on your light, so let your light be big and let it shine always. Study Leviticus 6:12-13, for it says, *"That the fire on the Levitical altar was never to go out."* Why? Because, fire always does something to itself and to something else. Dig deeper.

DAY 20

"Deer Sense"

As I sat in my tree stand, two deer approached the tree line. Walking with their heads to the ground, they were following an invisible deer, which happened to be me. The deceptive trail was one that I had made to bring them right to me. While they followed the trail, they would look for the usual signs of another deer, for they didn't just believe that they were totally right. Should we have as much sense as a deer? The deceptive trail appeared to be the travel route of another deer, but they still kept that wisdom in watching, as well as, doing other things. What happened to the deer? That's another story. Study Romans 8:12-17 and dig deeper.

☙DAY 21❧

"Pick One"

Inside every individual there are six people, but you must be the one to pick who you are. These are the choices. Number one, "who you are reputed to be". Number two, "who you are expected to be". Number three, "who you were". Number four, "who you wish to be". Number five, "who you think you are". Number six, "who you really are". Realize that you should never allow someone else to mold your world, it will always be too small for you. Who you really are is shown through time by the Holy Spirit, the experiences of life, and the desires of the heart which are constantly upgraded by the nature of Jesus in you. Read 2 Corinthians 5:12-20, as you dig deeper.

❧DAY 22❧

"Proper Focus"

A healthy mind is a mind whose eyes are in proper focus. Proper focus will allow you to see what's going on around you, as well as, what's going on ahead of you. When you strip your mind of illusions, pretenses, dishonesty, and pipe dreams, you get a look at life realistically. That's a mind that can defend against the wiles of evil people, as well as, evil spirits. Wisdom does great things through a clear mind. Study Romans 12:1-2, as you dig deeper.

☙DAY 23❧

"Sin is a Factory"

The power of sin is the reproduction of the products which come from a tainted nature. That reproduction sets many seeds in your life that causes a harvest of consequences beyond measure. The power of your mistake is the mirror-house of reminders. Every way you look, all you see is you. Then the guilt, a method of attack, makes you feel useless and worthless. Does that sound familiar in some cases? So, now you can believe God for anything, because you have no basis for your faith to operate, because sin has been working overtime in the factory. Shut the factory down, and build a new business based on renewing the mind. Read John 3:20-21, and as always, dig deeper.

❧DAY 24❧

"Getting Rid of Giants"

The Bible teaches us that there are two ways to deal with giants. Like David in 1 Samuel 17, we can knock them down, and then take the pleasure of cutting their head off, or we can be like Caleb and just eat them up as a good meal of victory. Caleb said that the giants are the Breakfast of Champions. Study Numbers 14:9, and as you dig deeper, believe for the wisdom that causes you to see the victory in every circumstance regardless of the size of the condition you face.

DAY 25

"Life's Little Interruptions"

When life doesn't go exactly the way you planned, don't get bent out of shape. Little interruptions can prepare you for greater service and greater victories. The Pit, Potiphar, and the King's Prison were interruptions in Joseph's life. But when we read the story, we see that they equipped him to assist Pharaoh in saving much of that known world. Just like you, that's right, I'm talking to you, Joseph wondered how his dreams would fare with all that was happening around him and to him. "But God", you can say that again, "But God". Right there was your answer, right there was your way-maker, right there, when you said, His name, you are calling on the One who can reverse the irreversible, and because our enemies try to do the unthinkable. Read Genesis chapter 37 through 45 and really dig deeper.

❧ DAY 26 ❧

"The New Birth"

The new birth is not just a birth, but a quickening, as we passed from death to life. It is a resurrection and it is also a creation. Once born-again, we are raised up with Him to walk in newness of life. Justification gives us a new standing, and regeneration gives us our new heart. In Christ, nothing is above us. Everything outside of Jesus is beneath us. Why? Because we are the Body of Christ in the earth, walking victorious in every situation, and leading humanity as world overcomers. There is a new nature in us that has made a pledge and a vow with the *"Law of the Spirit of Life in Christ Jesus"*. That is truly the grace message, for grace and truth came by Jesus Christ. Study John 8:23, as you dig deeper.

❧DAY 27❧

"Type I Pride"

The Bible gives us a picture of two types of pride. Galatians 6:4, says, *"that the key to a respected type of pride is to not compare ourselves to others rather than testing our own self-worth by comparison to others, we are encouraged to do a little self-examination."* When you measure yourself against the Bible and score well, we can congratulate ourselves, but never at the expense of someone else. Wisdom looks to others before it looks to itself. Don't forget to dig deeper.

❦ DAY 28 ❧

"Type II Pride"

The Bible points out the feeling of superiority that can stalk a Christian, because those who walk close to God can sometimes look down on others less spiritual. A prideful man or woman looks down on people and things, and of course, as long as, he or she is looking down, they can't see anything or anyone else.

Luke 18:9-14, shows how pride, an invisible sin, seeps in like water in sand on the beach. Seeking wisdom will cause all kinds of spiritual sight to take place, and the result of that spiritual sight will be the ability to always examine oneself against the pride that causes us to fall.

❦DAY 29❧

"The Real Challenge"

It's easy to ride through life when you're in the season of blessing, upon blessing. The real challenge in life is keeping the victory when your season of blessing has changed. Are you going to give in to despair when everything is not exactly right or complain and cause your season of despair to remain? No, don't do either one of those. Sometimes you have to shake yourself, that's right, shake yourself until you feel free of that which is trying to attach itself to you from the outside. Shake it off like Paul did the viper. The same God who is with you during the refreshing seasons is the same God who will be with you through every season. Always dwell in the land of doing good and feed on God's faithfulness, and He will give you the desires of your heart. Read 1 Kings 18:21-40, because you are already digging deeper.

❧DAY 30❧

"Staying Prepared"

My grandfather was a part-time farmer, and he was sensitive to certain times and seasonal changes of the year. Even though some spring days were as cold as winter days, he would make sure the ground was prepared for planting seed. Shorty, the name of his mule, was hooked to the plow, and there was no such thing as waiting for better weather. It is the same in spiritual life, and if you wait for better weather, you may miss your bumper crop of eternal blessings. In this faith walk, there's no such thing as a perfect time to do anything. Faith is now and wisdom walks with faith to become a dynamic dual of help along the way. Study 2 Timothy 4:2, as you dig deeper.

✵ DAY 31 ✵

"Saving the Elderly"

Most of the time we think that only the young people need to be ministered to for salvation. Do you ever think about all those elderly people who haven't been saved, who haven't even been talked to about the saving grace of our Lord Jesus Christ? Wisdom causes us to see that everyone needs Jesus. While it is true that an older person who doesn't know the Lord can become hardened to the good news as they get older, God's word is powerful enough to save anyone who will receive and act on it. There is no age limitation on the saving grace of the Lord Jesus Christ. Look for an elderly person that you can connect to for the Kingdom of God. Read Luke 15:10, while you have your spiritual shovel in your hand digging deeper.

❦DAY 32❧

"Blessed and Highly Favored"

When we accept Jesus as Lord and Savior, we are birthed into the heavenly family of Almighty God. In other words, we become a part of God's forever family. We become recipients of the resources of heaven, and as a joint heir with Christ Jesus and an heir of God the Father, we are highly favored and most blessed. In Numbers 23:20, we are told that whoever God blesses, those blessings cannot be reversed. How much more should we be walking in our irreversible blessings of God under a better covenant with better promises? Wisdom always leads us to that which is better. Study Hebrews 8:6, as you dig deeper.

⚘DAY 33⚘

"You're the One"

1 Corinthians 1:26-27, says that *"You are the one God would like to use."* No education, no special skills, or high level of training, can automatically place you in the special category. Because you have a heart for better and for the use of service to others, your heart has drawn God's attention. We can all confess that we are not exactly the best choice for the work, but we know that God will correct that, because He will shape all for the work, and He will fit you in the perfect suit for your perfect service. Give Him a willing heart, and He will give you the rest. He works in taking the foolish things, like us, and confounding the wise. Just think about Moses, David or Paul, as you dig deeper.

❧ DAY 34 ❧

"Turn Old Memories Around"

If you have ever looked back, you should see how much God has blessed you despite your mistakes. There is something in every memory that will give you a "mercy signature" signed by God himself. God shows us that, just because we had a bad start, and improper moment, or devastating disappointment, we can still have a great finish. Your life today is more than what happened yesterday. Why? Because, it is what you do with what happened yesterday that will cause all members to be turned around. Study Philippians 3:13, as you dig deeper.

☙DAY 35☙

"The Great "C" Word"

In Ephesians 4:25-32, we are called to communicate, which generates pleasantness with the Holy Spirit. To communicate is sort of like vomiting, you don't want to do it, but it feels good when you get it over. Maybe that picture will help you to see how important it is to communicate in all situations, whether comfortable or uncomfortable. The process of communication brings up things you've forgotten or need to be reminded of. Draw from the wisdom of Proverbs 18:21 and practice it. The light side of that scripture means preserving, rebuilding, refreshing and restoring. That's what communication does in every place that is needed and not rejected. Keep digging deeper.

❧DAY 36❧

"The God Kind of Faith"

Mark 11 teaches us to live by faith, and that according to what's in our heart that we believe. Faith will not work in an unforgiving and unbelieving heart. Our love must be the dominating, motivating force behind all operations of faith. We see from scriptures, that the greatest hindrances to the God kind of faith has been the ever popular me, myself, and no one else attitude. It takes the same amount of courage to sit down and listen to others, (for faith comes by hearing), as it does to stand up and always speak of yourself. The God kind of faith keeps our eyes on the one who gave the revelation that we apply to every situation.

❧ DAY 37 ❧

"A Bigger You"

Tomato seeds have an inward command to produce a stalk that's a thousand times bigger than the seed. The Word of God works by the same principle when sown into the heart. The Word will produce more blessings than you can imagine. Why? Because, *"the Lord is the author and the finisher of our faith"*. He is the creator of the principles that we live by, the principles of the Kingdom of God. This is why farmers plant seeds every spring, because they know that the little seed will bring forth many more blessings of increase. Each believer must understand that the value you place on anything is immediately revealed by the price you are willing to pay for it. Digging deeper into the Word shows the value you place on growing.

❦DAY 38❦

"The Ministry of Raising Children"

A child needs a parent's love more than money, an example more than words, time more than toys, and prayer instead of punishment. A parent who shoulders this responsibility will build the foundation for his or her children to lead productive lives when they become adults. If that time of teaching responsibility is missed, those children will become prisoners to lack of knowledge, which in turn gives authority to any who possess greater knowledge to rule over them. We see from Scripture that consequences are the chosen experiences of those who have elected to walk in their own way, but blessings surround those who trust in the Lord. Study Psalms 37, as you dig deeper.

DAY 39

"Prayer Big Prayer"

Your harvest is determined by what you sow, not by what you just desire according to Mark 11. Whatever we expect in life is often a direct result of what we desire, so Scripture teaches us to sow along with desire. We will always find that through wisdom a person is defined by the actions, not just by their beliefs. You can study that in James 1:22. We usually expect a lot and are never satisfied until we get our desires met. That is why faith, not emotions, is the order of this life that you and I have in the Kingdom. If you try to receive through unhealthy emotions, you will cause your expectations to crumble, and the result is a fading away from faith. Pray and expect things to change, but pray in faith big prayers, and learn to sow for what you are believing for just as the farmer does every spring. Dig deeper.

✥DAY 40✥

"Trying to Survive"

In Genesis we see that Adam lost his vision for life, his purpose for creation. Because of his loss vision he is now thrown into survival mode, and now becomes a slave to need, instead of the abundance he was created to live in. In Matthew 6:24, Jesus says, *"you will serve the master you trust to meet your needs."* In other words, there is no middle ground when it comes to living life here in this fallen world. You must either live by the Word of God, or you live by the word of those who are already slaves to poverty and lack. It is impossible to be promoted for your intentions, because promotion is the reward of productivity. Study Matthew 6:33, as you dig deeper.

☙DAY 41❧

"Showing the Utmost Respect"

My mother taught me to show the utmost respect when listening to the preaching of the Word of God on Sundays or whenever presented. To allow your mind to wander is to dishonor the privilege of creation that is given to our minds. Honor is shown not just by actions and words, but also in thoughts. To converse with someone while listening to the Word of God in whatever service it might be is to dishonor the one speaking, not to mention the Holy Spirit who is governing the service. The next time you're wondering why something isn't working for you, check out your lack of respect for God's message. Read 1 Timothy 4:13, as you dig deeper.

⁐DAY 42⁐

"Speak to The Rock"

Have you ever been impatient about waiting on God? Moses became impatient with the people, and it cost him a very important entrance into the promises of God. We know today through all the experiences that we have had, and others have had in life, that many have not entered into certain promises of God, because of impatience. Moses act was in direct disobedience to God's command, and it broke a picture that God has been preparing for all ages. The next time you become impatient, think of the possible damage that may occur to others, because of your actions. Read Exodus 17:6 and Numbers 20:7-8, as you dig deeper.

⚘DAY 43⚘

"A Trip to Heaven"

Hebrews 11:6, says that *"He that cometh to God must believe that He is, and that He is a rewarder of those who seek Him."* That Scripture is telling you and I that before we pack our bags to make the trip, make sure you are fueled with faith. You keep your faith as you would keep a plant, by rooting it into your life, and making it grow greater by attending to it. You can always depend on this principle of life that says what you do first determines what someone else will do next, because anything that is done will cause a response. Dig deeper.

DAY 44

"The Rewards of Sharing Sin"

We have shared many things with others throughout our lives, and I am sure you can recapture the moments. Many joys, tears, laughs, positive words and broken feelings have all been a part of the sharing toward others that we have fulfilled in life. Sharing another's sin goes against the Word of God. 1 Timothy 5:22, should be studied intently. Those who share in the sin of another will reap the same rewards, and how great are those rewards. I've seen the result of a lie my mother told over 40 years ago, and family members are still receiving the reward of that sin. Why? Because, they partook of that sin. Remember the mischief of sin? It separates you from the goodness of God that has been ordained for you. Dig deeper.

☙ DAY 45 ❧

"Sin, the Mischief Maker"

As stated earlier, there is a separation that this mischief maker causes. In Jeremiah 5:25, it is stated that the mischief of sin has caused some damaging things to occur. Sin hindered God's mercies and we know everyone needs mercies. It put a partition wall between God and the people, and caused God's face to be hid, which denotes great displeasure. Sin and its great consequences separates us from God, and so it separates us not only from all good, but unto all evil. Get the picture? Read John 8:32, as you are digging deeper.

ᘏᗢ DAY 46 ᘏᗢ

"A Time of War"

Ecclesiastics 3:8 says, there is an appointed time for war. God brought His people out of Egypt by an act of war, war against every false god that they trusted in. War, as a believer, gives grace to fight, new armor to wear, and the opportunity for victory. War releases strategies that enable us to plunder the enemy's holdings and create a pipeline to unknown favor. Revelation chapters 3 and 4, reveal that we are called overcomers, so it is important for every believer to recognize who they are, and not who you used to be. Wisdom says, "we can never change what we are unwilling to face, so surely it is a time of war." Dig deeper.

❧DAY 47❧

"The Supernatural Walk"

The easiest way to explain this is to know that God's presence is on your natural presence. Paul summed it up best when he said, *"This is why, for Christ's sake, I delight in weaknesses, in insults, in hardships, in persecutions, in difficulties. For when I am weak, then I am strong."* What is the price for being a superhero? Some may think you're strange, and some may think you've lost your mind. But like the TV character Superman, they will call upon you when help is needed. Why? Because they know there is a strength in you that is there only, because of the presence of God in your life. Read 1 Corinthians 2:4-5, and 2 Corinthians 12:10, as you are digging deeper.

❧ DAY 48 ❧

"Second Mile Realities"

M atthew 5:41, is a picture of Jesus speaking beyond the normal limits to help. He challenges us to be different. Why, because change takes place by those that are different. In the 1st mile, the one who asked for your help is in control, but in the 2nd mile that I help, I'm in control. According to Romans 12:20-21, *"we overcome evil by doing good for someone else"*. Their need is the 1st mile, but our going beyond their need is the 2nd mile. That's a great Revelation for our Christian mission as we all dig deeper.

⚘DAY 49⚘

"Second Mile Realities"
Part 2

By now you've read Matthew 5:41, and can see the benefits of going the 2nd mile. The Jews were forced to carry the Romans packs, and Jesus tells us that if we are forced to help, help in a way that will overcome the evil that is presented to us. The next principle of the same lesson is that, if I walked the first mile in obedience to the request of another, the second mile I walk I'm walking in obedience to Christ. That's where the greater blessings come from. Hope you got that! Dig deeper, I call you blessed.

❧ DAY 50 ☙

"The Processionary Caterpillars"

Killing time is, killing potential. We already know from Scripture that activity is not necessarily accomplishments, but there are many who have good intentions, but are never promoted. These particular caterpillars followed each other 24 hours a day, for six days. They walked around the saucer that was filled with food, the resource for life that they needed. They confused activity with accomplishment, and they all died. Procrastination is a tool used to hold us back, never allowing us to enter into the resources that actually give life. Procrastination is filled with distractions, deceptions and discouragements. Study, 1 Samuel 17, the knock-down, head removal, victory of David over Goliath, as you dig deeper.

❧DAY 51❧

"Lost Time"

When you choose to kill time, you begin to abort those gifts/callings that God placed within you. That is actually called procrastination. In today's society, everyone is on the move, moving backwards, forward, and even rocking in rocking chairs, as a motion of never getting anywhere. More time has been lost sitting in a La-Z-Boy that will never be recovered and has forfeited many opportunities. We should never confuse activity with accomplishment, for they are very different even though both have movement. Wisdom teaches us that you will never possess what you are unwilling to pursue. Study 1 Kings 17, to get the revelation the widow received as you dig deeper.

✺ DAY 52 ✺

"Renewing the Mind"

Romans 12:1-2, is a picture of an absolute principle that must be followed in order to live victorious in the Kingdom of God. Faith proves to the mind the reality of things that cannot be seen by the eyes of the body. Faith can help you see further, see more and see it before others even get a glimpse. What we talk about seeing through the eyes of faith pertains to the promises from the Lord. Renewing the mind causes faith, which always expects, verbalizes and reinforces what it desires through words that come from our heart, to live life above the ordinary. Scripture repeatedly shows us the importance of living by faith. That's what digging deeper is all about, renewing the mind that we might live life above the ordinary.

DAY 53

"Doorway to New Seasons"

Romans 8:32, gives a picture to you and I that if there had been a limit on the life that God wanted us to have, He would not have given us Jesus. What can the Lord deny us after giving us Jesus? No one would have even asked God for His Son, yet He freely gave Him. Why? Because, God desires to increase the miracles and the favor that we receive. He desires to increase the pleasures of life and the achievements we receive. Jesus is the way, the truth, and the life to every new season. Study Ephesians 3:20, as you dig deeper.

❧ DAY 54 ❧

"Open for Miracles"

Ecclesiastics 3:11, says, that God has made everything beautiful in his time. Have you ever tried it your way? Have you ever told the Lord how to do it your way? Where to do it? When to do it? What time it had to be done? No matter how many times you've prayed about your way, He always does it His way. He makes it beautiful, it stirs the highest response from the senses of the mind to its highest level. In other words, He always gives you better than your imagination and your knowledge could ask for. In 2 Kings 5, we read the story of Naaman, who wanted it done his way and in his own time. We see the end of the story that God gave Naaman better than what his imagination could have hoped for. His miracle gave him the flesh of the child even though he was a grown man. Isn't God wonderful. Dig deeper, I call you blessed.

❧DAY 55❧

"Open the Miracles"
Part 2

John 9:1-7, gives us a picture of how Jesus worked in unusual ways. If you follow the history of Jesus, He did things that were unusual, and sometimes baffling to the religious people. In this particular instance, He spit on the ground and made clay, and put it on the eyes of the blind man. He then tells a blind man to walk across town and wash in a pool of flowing water. Beautiful in his own time, beautiful in his own way, and beautiful in setting forth a permanent testimony of God's goodness. Later on, when asked to testify about Jesus, the man born blind that now see simply said, *"all I know is that before I was blind, but now I see"*. He declared Jesus to be a Prophet. There should always be that readiness to express God's goodness when receiving a miracle.

❦ DAY 56 ❦

"Open for Miracles"
Part 3

First Kings 17:8, begins the story of God sending his man to a city called Sidon. Remember how beautiful God does things? God could have sent angels, but He chose a widow lady. Who would have ever thought? Not the rich, or the great men of that area was the Prophet sent to, but to a widow that was in need. Fixing her last meal, knowing that there is nothing beyond that, hope is gone out of the door, and destruction is invited in. Read the story. It is God's way to make use of, and to put honor upon the week and the foolish things of this world. Dig deeper, there are many beautiful things in the workings of God.

⚘DAY 57⚘

"Promises Made by God"

Revelation 19:10, shares with every believer that the Holy Spirit inspires true prophecy. These are not predictions like a typical human being would make. Prophecies are statements that come from God's spokesman. Prophetic words are actually divine guarantees, that certain things will take place in the future. Why? How? Because, in His sovereignty, God is the active agent in fulfilling His promises. Wisdom would have us to look to the word of God for all the answers that we need in life, because as we just said, God is the active agent in fulfilling his promises. Study Isaiah 55:11, as you dig deeper.

⚜DAY 58⚜

"The Little Things"

In Acts 17:28, it reminds us that our total identity, significance, and self-worth rest in Jesus Christ. Little is much when God is in it, as Scripture has shown through each generation of men and women that God has used. David, though destined to rule in Zion, felt as insignificant as a flea when running from King Saul. Scripture says that Samuel had a little coat, not a big coat, but a little coat. The widow had a little cruise of oil. When Elijah prayed, his servant only saw a small hand that resembled a little cloud. Jesus only had a few loaves of bread and a few small fish, but yet, for the multitude. These are just some of the famous stories we know from the Bible that show little things, became much in the presence of God. So, don't despise insignificant things, because they can become great through the spirit of faith. We are still digging deeper.

ᘛDAY 59ᘚ

"The Little Things"
Part 2

In 1 Samuel 26:20, it reveals the picture of reproach that David had received from King Saul. David declares that Saul has come out seeking a flea as one hunting quail in the mountains. David saw himself as insignificant, as a parasite that flourish in the sand and in the dust, a flea. Fleas are always an isolated insect, and David felt isolated. David soon became a leader of leaders, because he followed principles of respect and dignity to God's laws. He became a world overcomer, even though at one time he felt as small as a flea. When David stayed in the place where God would always receive him, then the great changes in life came. It is no different today in the way Jesus works with us. It is not until He receives us, that He can change us. Receiving precedes change. Hope you got that as you keep digging deeper.

❧ DAY 60 ❧

"World Overcomers"

1 John 5:1-5, gives a picture of those who have a lifestyle of faith. We are world overcomers through our faith and set forth to be examples before all men. This lifestyle of faith requires us to respect the power of our tongues. Our tongues are one of our greatest gifts and should be used correctly. When God wanted to create creation, He spoke. We see that words are creative forces that bring into existence that which did not exist before. James 3:4-5, reveals that our tongues are very powerful instruments and should be used to produce life, and not death. In the country we used screen doors to prevent obnoxious insects from entering into our home. Your words are like spiritual screen doors, that prevent the obnoxious from entering into your life. Always speak faith and always believe for life. Keep digging deeper.

⚘DAY 61⚘

"World Overcomers"
Part 2

In Joshua 1:8, it gives the instruction that we are to talk to ourselves, and the talk should consist of what God has said. External communication is what you say to others when you are having conversation. Internal communication is what you say to yourself, *"for faith comes by hearing, and that by the Word of God"*. What you say about your future, enemy, or expectations will drastically affect you, because your words are affecting the spiritual realm. Always access your own atmosphere. Learn to diagnose the currents, climate and emotional atmosphere others are creating around you. When you access your own atmosphere, you will always keep the bugs out.

☙DAY 62❧

"World Overcomers"
Part 3

Matthew 6:9-13, is a direct communication from our Lord Jesus to His disciples, which includes us, about what God wants to hear. As an overcomer, we should say what God wants to hear. Why? Because God says what he believes, and because we have the same spirit of faith, we speak what we believe. You need to understand that your words do affect God, and so Jesus taught us to pray words that affect God. What were those words in this particular lesson? They are words of provision, protection, and pardon. This is why, it so important to renew the mind, that there may be agreement between the way God thinks, and the way we think. Keep digging deeper.

✤DAY 63✤

"World Overcomers"
Part 4

Matthew 10:22, says that we should focus on the rewards of finishing. Why? Because our faith overcomes the world. Every season, task or time, has an unpleasant side. Sometimes it seems as if they have both sides of the coin, but you must focus on the end results of your fruitful life. Complaining people only focus on the wrong things, the wrong effort, and the wrong responsibility. Champions talk faith, victory, and great rewards. Champions ask different questions than normal people do about situations. Remember David asking questions about Goliath? Read 1 Samuel 17:26, as you dig deeper. I call you blessed.

ᘓᗷDAY 64ᘗᘔ

"World Overcomers"
Part 5

In 1 John 4:4, it reveals that we have been born of God, unto God, and for God. So, it is important to understand that what you see and hear does affect your life for God. Stay away from people whose words are poison, destructive, and filled with doubt and unbelief. Refuse to play the role of the victim, for the victims' role is always that of lack. You have an anointing from God wrapped around you, and you are not a captive, because you have been set free. You are actually more than a conqueror, so you must keep your mind from being exhausted by a victims' vocabulary. What you see and hear will determine how you feel about things, and so as a world overcomer refuse any part of the victims' role.

⚘DAY 65⚘

"Avoiding Deception"

Luke 18:9-14, presents to us five particular features that we should avoid in life. Self-righteousness always creates spiritual blindness and in turn carries us off into deception. The first feature points to self-centeredness. The Pharisee was entirely self-centered, a key characteristic of self-righteousness. It is the common characteristic when dealing with particular demonic spirits. You notice that they pray with themselves. We see from Scripture that nearly every passage in the New Testament pertains to the end of the age which includes some kind of warning about being deceived. Wisdom would have us to know better and because no one is immune to being deceived, we must be able to identify truth to stay free. Are you still digging deeper?

✺❦DAY 66❧✺

"Avoiding Deception"
Part 2

Luke 18:9-14, is still the subject matter to cover these five features that are found in deception. Disdain for others is the next feature that leads to deception. The Pharisees felt superior to others, particularly to those close to them. Self-righteous people are so wrapped up in themselves that they degrade and devalue everyone else around them. Sounds familiar? Because, deception and pride are employed, we need to make sure we do not hire them, nor pay their wages for the destruction they bring into people's lives.

❧DAY 67☙

"Avoiding Deception"
Part 3

Luke 18:9-14, is our anchored Scripture base for this lesson. The next devastating feature that leads to deception is the comparison law of devaluing a person. The Pharisee thanked God for making him different from the tax collector. That kind of comparison is unscriptural. None of us are better than the other, but some of us just think better than others. If you have read this far, you already know that without Jesus none of us would be anything anyway. God does not compare us to others, nor does He condone that practice on our part. We are all called to be one, and if one, how can there be two? Dig deeper.

⚘DAY 68⚘

"Avoiding Deception"
Part 4

Luke 18:9-14, is helping us to see that the way up is to first go down. This fourth devastating feature characteristic of deception is the personalized set of rules that one lives by. The Pharisee used a tailor-made set of rules to justify his righteousness. Instead of a list of positive practices, he kept a list of negative behaviors he did not engage in. The fasting and tithing that he mentioned was to reinforce his righteousness, while all along he was using everything as a defense mechanism against truth. We know that man shall live by every word that proceeds out of the mouth of God. To be sure that you are dealing with truth, you must ask yourself three questions. Number one, is it true to Jesus? Number two, is it true to the Bible? Number three, is it witnessed by the Holy Spirit? Dig deeper.

❧DAY 69❧

"Avoiding Deception"
Part 5

Luke 18:9-14, will help every believer understand the importance of truth. Now we will cover the last feature characteristic of deception which is static righteousness. The Pharisees righteousness was completely static, allowing no room for change or progress. How sad, very sad. He intended to continue as usual, living in compliance to his little rule box, not expecting to improve, or to acknowledge that he needed to improve. Ever met people like that? Sure, you have. These are five features that are delivered to us by our Lord that we may understand the power of deception among those who should know the letter of the word. Thanks for digging deeper.

✤DAY 70✤

"Kingdom Confessions"

Hebrews 11:1, instructs us that faith is now. Now faith is, not tomorrow faith will be, but faith is now. Faith rests into dynamic places, in our heart and our mouth. Faith instructs us to put action to the things that we believe for, and in doing so, our heart faith and our mouth faith will produce that which we desire. This is not just naming something and claiming it from a carnal mind, but our confession is coming from our heart which is filled with the promise and will of God. Job 22:28, says that you shall decree a thing. What does decree mean? Speak words like architectural drawings that bring forth the desired result. Let's look at this some more as we dig deeper.

❧DAY 71❧

"Kingdom Confessions"
Part 2

Hebrews 11:1, cannot be nullified, nor changed. Your power to change circumstances is present with you every day if the word is being applied to your heart every day. John 2:1-11, is a lesson on how faith works. Faith has points of contact and instructions of action. The servants were instructed to draw the water, fill the pots, and carry the water made wine to the governor. Any part left out would have created failure to receive the benefit of divine request. When Jesus asked them to do it, He asked them to do it right then, because faith is now. The wedding was happening right now, and action had to happen right now to benefit the marriage ceremony. Hope you got that as you dig deeper?

☙DAY 72☙

"Kingdom Confessions"
Part 3

Hebrews 11:1, is a part of all Scripture, which cannot be nullified. Mountain moving faith is never quiet. It is aggressive, and it is right now. It is spoken, because you believe in your heart and confess with your mouth that any tangible object, substance, or invisible thing can become a testimony of God's goodness to us. In John 9:1, the story of the man born blind begins, and again points of contact and faith instructions followed by actions produced that which is never been done since the world began, the eyes of one born blind completely open to see. It is said that Jesus spit into the dust, made clay, put it in his eyes, gave him instructions to go find the pool, and wash. Again, I say that any part left out would have created failure. When did all this take place? Right now, do it, right now. Faith is now and so confession is now. Speak it now and put actions to that which you speak.

DAY 73

"Kingdom Confessions"
Part 4

Matthew 26:73, reveals to us that how we talk will reveal to others where we are in God. In other words, your speech will locate you. Knowing in advance that the seed you sow will grow after its own kind, that kind of faith talk will literally put you in control of your own destiny. When you sow the word, every wall, limitation or curse can be broken. Why? Because our faith flows from the heart of God who gave us the promises, and in turn watches over his word to perform it. As believers, we should always have a reputation for speaking truth in love. It's a different sound. Why? Because we tell it like it is. God can't lie, so our consistency is evidence of faithfulness and truthfulness.

⚇DAY 74⚇

"Kingdom Confessions"
Part 5

Galatians 4:6-7, says that the Spirit of the heir of all things has been sent into our hearts. Praise God, the Spirit of Jesus has been imparted into our hearts. This particular mantle that we received has been given that his life might be worked out and through us. As it is stated in Romans 1:16-17, we live from faith to faith. In other words, we grow out of the faith we have into new faith. Like outgrowing a pair shoes, we need a new pair. So, we need new faith to constantly grow free from condemnation, bitterness, revenge and self-pity. By the way, those are the devil's babysitters. Whenever we worry, we commit spiritual adultery. Why? Because, we try to join ourselves to another source of strength. Study the Song of Solomon as you dig deeper.

DAY 75

"Kingdom Confessions"
Part 6

G alatians 5:5-6, reveals to us that our faith is in Christ, and Christ is in us. This faith is energized by the new dimension of love. This faith, an unprecedented display of might and power through God, is activated and energized, expressed, and works through the love of God. Kingdom confessions are birthed from the love of God for us, and as He has spoken to us, we also speak. Our confessions bring things out of the shadows and into reality. So like God creates, restores and reproduces to the instruments of his Word, he's given us the same privilege through Kingdom confessions. Speak the Word as you dig deeper, I call you blessed.

❧ DAY 76 ❧

"The Bitter Taste of Revenge"

Genesis 50:20-21, and Matthew 6:14-15, will be the foundational basis for this particular wisdom principle. When we are hurt, it does not take long to find ourselves wanting payment, from those who are indebted to us. Hurt and offense will always ask questions like, "doesn't someone owe you something, like an apology or second chance?" The real question we should ask ourselves is that of what I'm thinking about. Is it justice that I'm seeking, or is it revenge that I have on my mind? Justice demands that those who do evil against society be punished by society. Revenge is a matter of the heart, for it speaks about getting even. Question your motives about why you do what you do and want what you want as you dig deeper.

❧DAY 77❧

"The Bitter Taste of Revenge"
Part 2

In Genesis 50:20-21, and Matthew 6:14-15, continues to reveal to us a principle of wisdom for our lives. Stop and think about it. We could all make a long list of disappointments, or traumatic events that others have bought into our lives. Your parents should have been more protective, or your children should have been more appreciative. Your spouse should have been more sensitive, or your preacher should have been more attentive. Because "Revenge" is a matter of the heart, Scripture tells us "to guard our hearts with all diligence". Do you think that there is someone who owes you an explanation or a fresh start? Maybe you are divorced, and you are still holding that offense, because someone threw away your marriage. Thinking about settling the score is always done at a great expense, your life. Dig deeper into the Scriptures, wisdom will set you free.

❦DAY 78❦

"The Bitter Taste of Revenge"
Part 3

Matthew 6:14, is part of our foundational base for this wisdom principle. You will notice that Jesus doesn't question the reality of herds or wounds, nor of disappointments or rejections. He does not doubt that you have been sinned against, nor does He doubt that the wounds might be deep. The issue with Him is not the existence of pain, but the treatment of that pain. I read the story once about a grizzly bear feeding on discarded camp food, and no other animal dared to draw near. Then a skunk walked up and took its place next to the bear. The bear didn't object. Why? He knew the cost of getting even. We should at least have bear sense while we dig deeper.

☙DAY 79❧

"The Bitter Taste of Revenge"
Part 4

Matthew 6:14, as a wisdom principle builds a foundation for us to stand on against revenge. If you have ever watched the old Westerns, you notice that bounty hunters travel alone. Why? Who wants to hang out with someone who settles scores for a living? If you hang out with the bounty hunter you may catch a stray bullet, because they are always firing off at someone. Settling a score of revenge will cost you relationally and it will cost you physically. Amos 3:3, is a picture of unity, not individuality. Why so much on the taste of revenge? Because, if you are to settle the score, you will never rest just like the bounty hunter. As recorded in Job 5:2, *"resentment kills a fool"*. You will wear yourself out trying to get even. Get the taste of bitterness out of your mouth, and out of your heart, because your enemy may never pay up, he will never agree to an apology, and he may never repent. Dig deeper.

DAY 80

"Laws of The Spirit Realm"

In Galatians 5:16 and Romans 7:22-25, 8:1-2, is where we will find our foundational Scriptures for this particular wisdom principle. These Scriptures deal with operating principles of God's Kingdom, and the power of governing spiritual laws that cause us to be successful in life. With spiritual law, we control the natural instead of being controlled by the natural. Walking in the Spirit is being governed by spiritual law. We are not struggling to get in the Spirit, for we already own the Spirit being born of God and for God. The Kingdom of God operates in faith and the Kingdom of Darkness operates in fear. Total opposites, so we must choose our path and choose wisely, because the consequences of each path are already established. Get out your shovel, we are going to dig deeper.

❦ DAY 81 ❧

"Laws of The Spirit Realm"
Part 2

In Romans 8:2, it reveals that there are two kinds of spiritual laws that govern the spiritual dimensions. Paul talks about the "Law of the Spirit of Life in Christ Jesus" that has set us free from the "Law of Sin and Death". We know from life experience, and the wisdom that has been revealed to us, that these laws work when they are applied to our lives. Spiritual law is fulfilled in us who walk not after the flesh, but after the Spirit of Christ Jesus. We know the other law works from day to day in those who refuse to live in truth. One law produces life and peace, the other produces death. Wisdom always says, "choose life". Walking in the Law of the Spirit of Life is tied to our heart relationship with the Lord. For God's goodness surrounds us wherever we are.

❧DAY 82❧

"Laws of the Spirit Realm"
Part 3

Romans 8:3-8, is revealed to us so that the work of deception will not work. Deception tries to confuse the formula of walking in the spirit realm successfully. Spiritual forces are born in the human spirit at the time of the new birth. Galatians 5:22-23 declares that there is no law against these forces. Love, joy, peace, long-suffering, gentleness, goodness and faith are a part of every believer at birth. If not understood, the enemy would bring first-class disobedience to the workings of God. These are some of the spiritual forces that dematerialize the hidden counterfeits within our lives. Salvation is progressive as we dig deeper.

❧ DAY 83 ❧

"Laws of the Spirit Realm"
Part 4

In Galatians 5:16-25, it helps us to understand the major forces that are within a born-again believer. Faith, righteousness, wisdom, and love are all a part of every believer. The faith that we have is not a product of reason, but a part of our divine anatomy at the time of our conversion. This proves that the environment of walking in the spirit can be taken with you wherever you go. Why? Because, the just shall live by faith. It is not tied to a particular location, and it is definitely not tied to circumstances. Walking by faith, living righteous, having the right wisdom, and living forth in love is who we are, not who we are trying to become. Dig deeper.

⟡DAY 84⟡

"Divine Order"

In Romans 12:1-2, it revealed the steps to renew our minds. Wisdom says "that man should live by every word that proceedeth out of the mouth of God". Let's agree with wisdom. Here we see that the first step in renewing our minds is to present our bodies to the Lord Jesus Christ. He is the altar of sacrifice, and when we present ourselves to Him, He begins to help us think entirely different. In thinking differently, you live differently. You no longer conform to the world, but you are transformed in your behavior. Now we get into the good stuff as we dig deeper.

❧DAY 85❧

"Divine Order"
Part 2

Romans 12:1-2, carries us into the steps of being able to successfully follow divine order in having the mind of Christ. Once we have surrendered our bodies to Christ, which is our reasonable service, we find that God's will for us has been revealed to our renewed mind. Why? As we read earlier, because our behavior has changed. We discover God's will progressively through three distinct stages: good, acceptable, and perfect. As you get a revelation of God's will for your life, you will find that you have the faith needed to do His will. Why? Faith is a part of your birth nature in Christ Jesus. You have the appropriate faith required for the season of life that you occupy.

✥DAY 86✥

"Divine Order"
Part 3

In Romans 12:1-2, it helps us to follow the logical order of finding our place in the Body of Christ. As you discover God's will, you find your place and the particular function in the Body of Christ. You discover what member you are, and how you are to operate as that particular member. God is the one who gives gifts and those gifts are not conditional loans. We can use them properly, or we can fail to use them and therefore, lose them. But always remember this, Jesus said, *"you shall know them by their fruits"*, not by their gifts. Renewing the mind is the divine order that keeps us from doing things the world's way, looking like the world, and acting like the world. Dig deeper.

DAY 87

"Heart-to-Heart"

I Peter 3:7, lays out a unique picture for those who are married. Scripture says that we are to live as heirs together of the grace of life. In other words, a married state should be a state of rest. That's right, a marriage state should give rest to all the wondering affections, and through the marriage those affections are then fixed. When affections are fixed, the heart should be at rest. When the heart is at rest, it constantly gains strength for other positions to be occupied in the Kingdom. This is why we dig deeper into all the Scriptures, for many do not understand that marriage should give rest to their hearts. I call you blessed.

☙ DAY 88 ❧

"Divine Opportunities"

In Isaiah 55:9, it brings us to a revelation of why we can trust God. He does not see things the way we see them, nor does he think about them the way we think about them. There is nothing that God is not supernatural in. Outside of the supernatural, He cannot be defined, so we must never limit Him to ourexperiences, wisdom, culture, or our surroundings. He brings us favor through the promises of the word. That can be external favor, which is always by association and it carries with it an expiration date. Then there is direct favor, that comes when you are in your right lane knowing who you are, and because you know who you are your abilities are magnified. Let's dig deeper into this much-needed lesson of wisdom.

⚛️DAY 89⚛️

"Divine Opportunities"
Part 2

Isaiah 55:9 reveals to us God's way of thinking, and the opportunities we have, because we are connected to his will. Because we are connected to his will, opportunities are actually looking for those of us who pursue destiny. Opportunities require your ability to reach, as taught in Mark 5:25. When we pursue opportunities it causes us to stretch. There are also opportunities that pursue us, such as Jesus and Zacchaeus. One big point to remember about divine opportunities is that timing is most important. Some opportunities come only once-in-a-lifetime as blind Bartimaeus understood. Digging deeper.

☜DAY 90☞

"Divine Opportunities"
Part 3

In 2 Kings 4:1-7, it is one of the famous stories listed about divine opportunities. We see in the short set of verses that the oil was to be multiplied in the pouring. Because of obedience in carrying out the instructions given in this time of opportunity, the part of oil, like a fountain of living water, was always flowing yet always full. The second set of instructions in this divine opportunity reveals to the widow to sell the oil to the rich and pay off the debt. You notice how divine opportunities give directions and connections in the right time. The insignificant can become very significant through divine opportunities received. You notice her faith was tied to the conclusion, not the beginning. Hope you got that as you dig deeper.

≈DAY 91≈

"Signs of the End Time"

In Luke 17:26, is a sure word given by our Lord Jesus Christ about the end time. *"As it was in the Days of Noah"*, says Jesus, *"so it will be in the last days before his appearance."* Evil thoughts, violence, sexual perversion, evil intervention, false prophets, false church, disobedient, and even misplaced love are all signs like in the Days of Noah. The first spiritual manifestation in human history of the antichrist was brought forth in Jesus' day in the form of Barabbas. A murderer, chosen to be with the people instead of a Savior. False prophets will increase in times of spiritual decline, because from them come predictions that contradict the Word of God. Wisdom gives us spiritual sight to see the signs already surrounding this world. Dig deeper.

✥DAY 92✥

"Generational Wealth"

In Matthew 6:19-20, it gives a picture of how important wealth is. Sometimes wealth disturbs people, but those of the kingdom mindset, a renewed mind, understands that wealth is something that we are, and riches are things that we have. Wealth will pass through death, but riches will not. Why? We became Sons of God when we were born again, which gives us the relationship with Him as our father, and as our Father He is Lord of heaven and earth. So, our wealth flows from our bloodline, and the riches flow from what we obtain in life. So, you and I as believers have been born into time wealth, revelational wealth, and material wealth. If owning things is a sin, that would make God the chief of sinners. Ridiculous! Ridiculous! Dig deeper, for you are part of God's forever family.

☙DAY 93☙

"Bible Economics"

In 1 Peter 2:9, it declares that you and I are part of a chosen generation. In other words, there are no second-class citizens in the Kingdom of God. We are spirit-filled and spirit-directed, and God as property owner and manager directs us in planning, strategic objectives, productivity, and accountability. These are all skills to operate the world of property and the world of souls. Rather than rejecting the material world and the management of it, God ordains it. Matthew 6:10, declares *"on earth as it is in heaven,"* which reveals that God incarnates his spiritual ideas into the natural world. We are a chosen generation to receive such great blessings. Dig deeper, for wisdom is the principal thing.

❧DAY 94❧
"Principles of the Mind"

In Matthew 8:5-13, it reveals one of the dynamic principles of the mind called "belief". Whatever you believe with strong convictions becomes your reality. Your lifestyle does not reveal what you have been taught, it reveals what you believe. People always establish paradigms, which are well-traveled paths, that are easy to walk on, but they always lead to the same destination. Psychologists say it takes 3 to 5 weeks to create a new thought pattern. Even 95% of your beliefs are programmed by age 13. That alone is enough proof of why we need to renew our minds with the Word of God. Let's dig deeper.

DAY 95

"Principles of the Mind"
Part 2

In 2 Corinthians 10:3-6, it reveals to us another principle of the mind called "substitution". Your mind can only hold one thought at a time, and you can substitute one thought with another. Thus, we have the principle of substitution. There are beliefs, values, identity and even expectations that sometimes need to be substituted with another thought. This power "substitution" causes us to replace the disappointments in our minds with life-giving issues for the future. The mind is a powerful thing and you should understand its abilities to be successful in life. Digging deeper.

DAY 96

"Principles of The Mind"
Part 3

In Job 22:28, it brings a revelation to us of another principle of the mind called expectation. We declare what we expect to happen and so whatever you expect with confidence becomes your own self-fulfilling prophecy. Jesus used this particular principle, when speaking to the fig tree. What He expected to happen to the fig tree immediately began to happen. The power of faith and expectation will break the mental prisons as a renewed mind is forged.

DAY 97

"Our Decisions"

Kings 7:3-10, is a lesson in how to set forth our destiny. We see the "decisions" of these men determined their destiny, not their conditions. That's right, decisions, not conditions, determine your destiny. Your decisions have pre-determined outcomes. In other words, the choices that you make are like witnesses in the courtroom of consequences. Proverbs 23:6-7, gives us more insight into the power of making decisions, for as we think in our heart, that's what we become, that's what we have, and that's what life will be.

❦DAY 98❧

"Principles of the Seed"

In Genesis 8:22, it reveals God's ordained plan for our resources. The seed was given to man in order to unlock the hidden doors of provision and abundance. In other words, the seed has a set assignment. Everything in your life will be created by a seed that has purpose, that has a set assignment, that has an ordained harvest. Your seed will act as a passport into future abundance for you, but you must remember that it's only a seed until its sown. Dig deeper.

DAY 99

"Principles of the Seed"

In Luke 6:38, it brings the insight of the Lord Jesus into our resources. He reveals that the measure of the seed we sow determines the size of the harvest we reap. In other words, what's in the seed is better than the seed. The spiritual rule is totally opposite for those who do not sow. A seed never sown will produce a harvest never grown, according to Galatians 6:9. Study the seed principles if you desire to be a great giver in the Kingdom of God and always dig deeper.

❧DAY 100❧

"Faith for Impossible Situations"

In Hebrews 11, we see the revelations of the importance of living by faith, which pleases God. Faith causes great rewards to come even in impossible situations. There is a list of names recorded in the "Faith Hall of Fame". The Bible is not just about God, but it is also about the people that trusted God. They trusted in God in the same way that students tend to internalize the beliefs that teachers have about their ability. Generally, students rise or fall to the level of expectations of their teachers. When teachers believe in students, students believe in themselves. Students tend to give to teachers, as much, or as little as teachers expect of them. With all that said… There is no difference between the way students behave toward their teachers and how we behave toward God. If we trust God, we know he has said certain things about our ability as believers. He believes that we are more than conquerors, and we should believe in ourselves, because *greater is he who lives in us than he who lives in the world*".